The End of a Perfect Day

THOMAS KINKADE

HARVEST HOUSE PUBLISHERS

EUGENE, OREGON

The End of a Perfect Day

Text Copyright © 2002
by Media Arts Group, Inc., Morgan Hill, CA 95037 and
Harvest House Publishers, Eugene OR 97402

Published by Harvest House Publishers
Eugene, OR 97402

ISBN 0-7369-0633-9

Verses are taken from: the Holy Bible, New International Version®.
Copyright © 1973, 1978, 1984 by the International Bible Society.
Used by permission of Zondervan Publishing House;
and the King James Version of the Bible.

Design and production by Koechel Peterson & Associates,
Minneapolis, Minnesota

Printed in Hong Kong

02 03 04 05 06 07 08 09 10 11 / NG / 10 9 8 7 6 5 4 3 2 1

A well-spent day brings happy sleep.

~ LEONARDO DA VINCI

Peace and rest at length have come
   All the day's long toil is past,
And each heart is whispering,
   "Home, Home at last."

— THOMAS HOOD

Bend low, O dusky Night,

   And give my spirit rest,

   Hold me to your deep breast,

And put old cares to flight.

Give back the lost delight

   That once my soul possest,

   When Love was loveliest.

— LOUISE CHANDLER MOULTON

*H*ushed in the smoky haze of summer sunset,
When I came home again from far-off places,
How many times I saw my western city
    Dream by her river.

Then for an hour the water wore a mantle
Of tawny gold and mauve and misted turquoise
Under the tall and darkened arches bearing
    Gray, high-flung bridges.

Against the sunset, water-towers and steeples
Flickered with fire up the slope to westward,
And old warehouses poured their purple shadows
    Across the levee.

High over them the black train swept with thunder,
Cleaving the city, leaving far beneath it
Wharf-boats moored beside the old side-wheelers
    Resting in twilight.

— SARA TEASDALE
"SUNSET"

To go fishing is the chance to wash one's soul with pure air, with the rush of the brook, or with the shimmer of sun on blue water. It brings meekness and inspiration from the decency of nature, charity toward tackle-makers, patience toward fish, a mockery of profits and egos, a quieting of hate, a rejoicing that you do not have to decide a darned thing until next week.

— HERBERT HOOVER

All those golden autumn days
the sky was full of wings. Wings
beating low over the blue water
of Silver Lake, wings beating high
in the blue air far above it . . .
bearing them all away to the green
fields in the South.

~ Laura Ingalls Wilder

A perfect summer day is when
the sun is shining, the breeze
is blowing, the birds are singing,
and the lawn mower is broken.

— JAMES DENT

Some people are

making such thorough

plans for rainy days

that they aren't enjoying

today's sunshine.

— WILLIAM FEATHER

13

A twilight like blue dust sifted into the shallow fold of the thickly wooded hills. It was early October, but a crisping frost had already stamped the maple trees with gold, the Spanish oaks were hung with patches of wine red, the sumac was brilliant in the darkening underbrush. A pattern of wild geese, flying low and unconcerned above the hills, wavered against the serene ashen evening.

— SINCLAIR LEWIS

God saw all that he had made,

and it was very good.

— THE BOOK OF GENESIS

I do not ask to walk smooth paths
Nor bear an easy load.
I pray for strength and fortitude
To climb the rock-strewn road.

Give me such courage I can scale
The hardest peaks alone,
And transform every stumbling block
Into a steppingstone.

– GAIL BROOK BURKET

No matter how

sophisticated you

may be, a huge

granite mountain

cannot be denied—

it speaks in silence

to the very core

of your being.

– Ansel Adams

*I*f you observe a really happy man you will find him building a boat, writing a symphony, educating his son, growing double dahlias in his garden, or looking for dinosaur eggs in the Gobi desert. He will not be searching for happiness as if it were a collar button that has rolled under the radiator. He will not be striving for it as a goal in itself. He will have become aware that he is happy in the course of living life twenty-four crowded hours of the day.

— W. BERAN WOLFE

God called the light "day," and the darkness he called "night." And there was evening, and there was morning—the first day.

— THE BOOK OF GENESIS

Drop a pebble in the water,
And its ripples reach out far;
And the sunbeams dancing on them
May reflect them to a star.

Give a smile to someone passing,
Thereby making his morning glad;
It may greet you in the evening
When your own heart may be sad.

Do a deed of simple kindness;
Though its end you may not see,
It may reach, like widening ripples,
Down a long eternity.

— JOSEPH NORRIS

$\mathcal{A}$ happy life is not built up of tours abroad and pleasant holidays, but of little clumps of violets noticed by the roadside, hidden away almost so that only those can see them who have God's peace and love in their heart; in one long continuous chain of little joys, little whispers from the spiritual world, and little gleams of sunshine on our daily work.

— EDWARD WILSON

Climb the mountains and get their good tidings. Nature's peace will flow into you as sunshine flows into trees. The winds will blow their own freshness into you, and the storms their energy, while cares will drop off like autumn leaves.

– JOHN MUIR

23

My heart,
    The sun hath set.
Night's paths
    With dews are wet.

Sleep comes
    Without regret;
Stars rise
    When sun is set.

All's well.
    God loves thee yet,
Heart, smile,
    Sleep sweet, nor fret.

      – WILLIAM QUAYLE

The smiling Spring comes in rejoicing,
  And surly Winter grimly flies;
Now crystal clear are the falling waters,
  And bonie blue are the sunny skies.
Fresh o'er the mountains breaks forth the morning,
  The ev'ning gilds the ocean's swell;
All creatures joy in the sun's returning,
  And I rejoice in my bonie Bell.

The flowery Spring leads sunny Summer,
  The yellow Autumn presses near;
Then in his turn comes gloomy Winter,
  Till smiling Spring again appear:
Thus seasons dancing, life advancing,
  Old Time and Nature their changes tell;
But never ranging, still unchanging,
  I adore my bonie Bell.

→ ROBERT BURNS

O Paradise! O Paradise!
 Who doth not crave for rest?
 Who would not seek the happy land
 Where they that love are blest?

— FREDERICK WILLIAM FABER

What we are left with then is the present, the only time where miracles

happen. We place the past and the future as well into the hands of God.

The biblical statement that "time shall be no more" means that we will

one day live fully in the present, without obsessing about past or future.

— MARIANNE WILLIAMSON

Return unto thy rest, my soul,
 From all the wanderings of thy thought,
From sickness unto death made whole,
 Safe through a thousand perils brought.

— JAMES MONTGOMERY

*I*f any little thought of ours

Can make one life the stronger;

If any cheery smile of ours

Can make its brightness longer;

Then let us speak that thought today,

With tender eyes aglowing,

So God may grant some weary one

Shall reap from our glad sowing.

— Author unknown

Rest and be thankful.

— An inscription on
a stone seat on the
top of one of the
Highlands in Scotland

31

Why leap the fountains from their cells
Where everlasting Bounty dwells?—
That, while the Creature is sustained,
His God may be adored.

Cliffs, fountains, rivers, seasons, times—
Let all remind the soul of heaven;
Our slack devotion needs them all;
And Faith—so oft of sense the thrall,
While she, by aid of Nature, climbs—
May hope to be forgiven.

— WILLIAM WORDSWORTH

*I*t was one of those brooding, changeful days that come between Indian summer and winter, when the leaf colors have grown dim and the clouds come and go among the cliffs like living creatures looking for work: now hovering aloft, now caressing rugged rock-brows with great gentleness, or, wandering afar over the tops of the forests, touching the spires of fir and pine with their soft silken fringes as if trying to tell the glad news of the coming of snow… After this grand show the cloud-sea rose higher, wreathing the Dome, and for a short time submerging it, making darkness like night, and I began to think of looking for a campground in a cluster of dwarf pines. But soon the sun shone free again, the clouds, sinking lower and lower, gradually vanished, leaving the Valley with its Indian-summer colors apparently refreshed, while to the eastward the summit-peaks, clad in new snow, towered along the horizon in glorious array.

— JOHN MUIR
"*THE YOSEMITE*"

A heart at peace
gives life to the body...

— THE BOOK OF PROVERBS

I will lie down and

sleep in peace, for you

alone, O LORD, make

me dwell in safety.

— THE BOOK OF PSALMS

What, but thee Sleep? Soft closer of our eyes!

Low murmurer of tender lullabies!

Light hoverer around our happy pillows!

Wreather of poppy buds, and weeping willows!

Silent entangler of a beauty's tresses!

Most happy listener! when the morning blesses

Thee for enlivening all the cheerful eyes

That glance so brightly at the new sun-rise.

— JOHN KEATS

In those vernal seasons of the year, when

the air is calm and pleasant, it were an

injury and sullenness against Nature not

to go out and see her riches, and partake

in her rejoicing with heaven and earth.

— JOHN MILTON

The summits, sketched upon the morning mist, now stood boldly forth, mountains of purple.

Old King Whiteface towered loftier than ever, and I registered a vow to dare his summit, at some future period of my trip.

Suddenly, a pool nearby was wrinkled as with a myriad of waterflies; a humming in the woods began and soon a sunshower sparked the air.

— ALFRED BILLINGS STREET
WOODS AND WATERS

My Daily Prayer

If I can do some good today,
If I can serve along life's way,
If I can something helpful say,
  Lord, show me how.

If I can right a human wrong,
If I can help to make one strong,
If I can cheer with smile or song,
  Lord, show me how.

If I can aid one in distress,
If I can make a burden less,
If I can spread more happiness,
  Lord, show me how.

— GRENVILLE KLEISER

Just for today, I will try to live through this day only, and not tackle my whole life problems at once. I can do something for twelve hours that would appall me if I felt that I had to keep it up for a lifetime.

Just for today, I will be happy. This assumes to be true what Abraham Lincoln said, that "most folks are as happy as they make up their minds to be."

Just for today, I will try to strengthen my mind. I will study. I will learn something useful. I will not be a mental loafer. I will read something that requires effort, thought, and concentration.

Just for today, I will adjust myself to what is, and not try to adjust everything to my own desires. I will take my "luck" as it comes, and fit myself to it.

Just for today, I will exercise my soul in three ways: I will do somebody a good turn, and not get found out. I will do at least two things I don't want to do—just for exercise. I will not show anyone that my feelings are hurt; they may be hurt, but today I will not show it.

Just for today, I will be agreeable. I will look as well as I can, dress becomingly, talk low, act courteously, criticize not one bit, not find fault with anything and not try to improve or regulate anybody except myself.

Just for today, I will have a program. I may not follow it exactly, but I will have it. I will save myself from two pests: hurry and indecision.

Just for today, I will have a quiet half hour all by myself, and relax. During this half hour, sometime, I will try to get a better perspective of my life.

Just for today, I will be unafraid. Especially I will not be afraid to enjoy what is beautiful, and to believe that as I give to the world, so the world will give to me.

— KENNETH L. HOLMES

Prayer at Eventide

I bring thee now, O God, the parcel of a completed day. For I have wrapped it in my thoughts, tied it with my acts, and stored it in the purposes for which I live.

As the evening falls and while I seek thy face in prayer, grant unto me the joy of good friends, the curative power of new interests and the peace of the quiet heart.

Bestow upon me, Eternal Spirit, light as darkness comes . . .

Light not of the sun but of the soul, not for the eye but for the mind.

Light by which to judge the errors and the wisdom of the day's work.

Light for the path that the soul must find in the tangled ways of coming days.

And grant thou again the healing touch of sleep.

— PERCY ROY HAYWARD

Paintings